The Edcamp Model

CORWIN CONNECTED EDUCATORS SERIES

The Edcamp Model

*Powering Up
Professional Learning*

The Edcamp Foundation

CORWIN
A SAGE Company

CORWIN
A SAGE Company

FOR INFORMATION:

Corwin

A SAGE Company

2455 Teller Road

Thousand Oaks, California 91320

(800) 233-9936

www.corwin.com

SAGE Publications Ltd.

1 Oliver's Yard

55 City Road

London EC1Y 1SP

United Kingdom

SAGE Publications India Pvt. Ltd.

B 1/I 1 Mohan Cooperative Industrial Area

Mathura Road, New Delhi 110 044

India

SAGE Publications Asia-Pacific Pte. Ltd.

3 Church Street

#10-04 Samsung Hub

Singapore 049483

Copyright © 2014 by Corwin

Printed in the United States of America.

A catalog record of this book is available from the Library of Congress.

ISBN 978-1-4833-7195-5

This book is printed on acid-free paper.

Executive Editor: Arnis Burvikovs

Associate Editor: Ariel Price

Production Editor: Amy Schroller

Copy Editor: Janet Ford

Typesetter: C&M Digitals (P) Ltd.

Proofreader: Susan Schon

Cover and interior design: Janet Kiesel

Marketing Manager: Lisa Lysne

Certified Chain of Custody
SUSTAINABLE Promoting Sustainable Forestry
FORESTRY www.sfiprogram.org
INITIATIVE SFI-01268

SFI label applies to text stock

14 15 16 17 18 10 9 8 7 6 5 4 3 2 1

Contents

Preface

Welcome to the Connected Educators Series.

The past few years have provided momentous changes for educators: Whether it's the implementation of the Common Core State Standards, educational innovations due to technology, teacher and administrator evaluations, or budget cuts, what is clear is that educational reforms come in different shapes and sizes. For many connected educators, one of the invaluable group support systems essential during these times is the professional learning network, also known as our PLN.

Our PLN can provide innovative ideas, current resources, and sound educational practices that stretch our thinking in ways we haven't yet experienced. Equally as important as how a PLN can professionally expand our horizons, it introduces new friends that we look forward to meeting in person. This Connected Educator Series brings together some important members of my PLN. These are educators with a depth of knowledge and level of experience that helps me stay current and up-to-date with my educational practices.

In this series, my book, *Flipping Leadership Doesn't Mean Reinventing the Wheel,* takes the innovative idea of flipping classrooms and presents it at the school leader level, engaging the school community in new and innovative ways. In *Connected Leadership,* Spike Cook shares his experiences moving from a novice to digital leadership and illustrates how other educators can do the same.

Digital experts, Steven Anderson and Tom Whitby, help increase your digital experience by using Twitter to locate a PLN to engage in daily professional development. In *The Relevant Educator,* Tom and Steven provide a plethora of tools to use, and define each and every one. Using those same tools, in their book *The Power of Branding,* Tony Sinanis and Joe Sanfelippo help you to brand your school in order to create a positive focus on the learning happening within the four walls. In his book, *All Hands on Deck,* Brad Currie offers us ways to engage with families and students using old techniques with new innovative approaches.

In *Teaching the iStudent,* Mark Barnes provides insight into the life and mind of the iStudent, and in *Empowered Schools, Empowered Students,* Pernille Ripp focuses on em**power**ing students and teachers. Also in the series, in *Diversity and Connected Learning,* Rafranz Davis shows how equity and diversity is vital to the social media movement, and why that is so important to education as we move forward.

Kristen Swanson from the Edcamp Foundation not only focuses on why the Edcamp model is a new innovative way to provide excellent professional development, but also explains how you can create an Edcamp in your school district in *The Edcamp Model: Powering Up Professional Learning.*

The books in the Connected Educator Series are designed to read in any order, and each provides information on the tools that will keep us current in the digital age. We also look forward to continuing the series with more books from experts on connectedness.

As Michael Fullan has said for many years, technology is not the right driver, good pedagogy is. The books in this connected series focus on practices that lead to good pedagogy in our digital age. To assist readers in their connected experience, we created the Corwin Connected Educators companion website (www.corwin.com/connectededucator) where readers can connect with the authors and find resources to help further their experience. It is our hope and intent to meet you where you are in your digital journey, and elevate you as educators to the next level.

Peter M. DeWitt, EdD @PeterMDeWitt

About the Edcamp Foundation

Built on principles of connected and participatory learning, Edcamp strives to bring educators together to talk about the things that matter most to them: teaching and learning. With schedules built by attendees on the day of the event, anyone in attendance at an Edcamp can facilitate a session, share their learning openly, or ask thoughtful questions.

Edcamps are

- free
- noncommercial and conducted with a vendor-free presence
- hosted by any organization interested in furthering the Edcamp mission
- made up of sessions that are determined on the day of the event
- events where anyone who attends can be a presenter
- reliant on the "rule of two feet" that encourages participants to find a session that meets their needs

The first Edcamp was held in May of 2010 by a group of educators in Philadelphia. Since then, there have been over 500 Edcamp events held in dozens of countries. In December 2011, the original founders of the Edcamp movement (and the authors of this text!) established the Edcamp Foundation to assist Edcamp organizers and support the growing community of Edcampers. All of the proceeds from this book go to fund the efforts of the Edcamp Foundation in their mission to "build and support a community of empowered learners."

This book is written by lead author Kristen Swanson and the other founding members of Edcamp.

 **Kristen Swanson, EdD,** helps teachers design meaningful interactive curricula at the local and national level. She has taught at the elementary level, served as a regional consultant for Response to Intervention (a school-based, multi-level prevention system to maximize student achievement and reduce behavior problems), and worked as an educational technology director for a public school district in Pennsylvania. She holds a BA degree from DeSales University, two MA degrees from Wilkes University, and an EdD degree from Widener University. Kristen is currently an adjunct in the DeSales University instructional technology MEd program and a senior research leader for BrightBytes, a data analytics platform that measures and links the use of technology to learning outcomes.

In addition to her experience as an educator, Kristen is also passionate about meaningful professional learning. She currently serves as a member of the Edcamp Foundation Board, and is the chair of the longstanding Edcamp Foundation Partner Program. She has shared her ideas and expertise at ASCD (Association for Supervision and Curriculum Development) conferences, TEDxPhiladelphiaEd, TEDxNYED, and Educon. She is also published in academic journals, including *Literacy Learning: The Middle Years* and the *Journal of Reading, Writing, and Literacy*. She is the author of *Professional Learning in the Digital Age: The Educator's Guide to User-Generated Learning, Unleashing Student Superpowers,* and *Teaching the Common Core Speaking and Listening Standards*.

Kristen is active in the educational technology sphere. She is a Google Certified teacher, Twitter teacher, Edublog award nominee, and avid blogger. She strongly believes that rigorous curriculum fosters meaningful technology integration, and she is also interested in the learning opportunities provided by asynchronous learning.

This book is dedicated to all Edcampers everywhere.
You have transformed an idea into a movement.

Learning Is Changing. Is Your PD Keeping Pace?

Since the advent of the Internet in 1997, things have changed. A lot. Learning used to be isolated and linear. Access to knowledge used to be limited, and experts were seldom available when needed. Today, however, the Internet has fashioned a learning environment with boundless access to information and people. In short, learning has become *connected*.

Will Richardson and Rob Mancabelli (2011) discuss the shift to connected learning in their groundbreaking text on Personal Learning Networks (PLNs), stating "We now have two billion potential teachers and the sum of human knowledge at our fingertips" (p. 542).

The consequences of connected learning permeate every aspect of our lives. We can now learn about new music recommendations from Pandora, visit almost any place in the world instantly via Google Earth, or widen our perspective by watching online videos from leaders in every field. Knowledge and experts are "on demand" every second of every day. And that's just the beginning.

Alarmingly, many schools aren't able to keep pace with these shifts. Millions of students around the world attend schools that continue to offer learning experiences that treat both knowledge and teachers as scarce resources. With each passing day, schools that fail to embrace connected learning become increasingly irrelevant and ineffective.

SO, WHY ARE SO MANY SCHOOLS STRUGGLING TO MAKE THIS CHANGE?

Well, it's important to remember that radical change in any field is hard (Dufour & Marzano, 2011). Transforming a system that's remained largely unchanged for over 100 years isn't easy. There are also a host of complex factors that contribute to a school's ability to redefine learning.

However, mounting research reveals that a critical element slowing the learning revolution in schools is **ineffective professional development for teachers**. If we don't model connected learning experiences for teachers, then it's unlikely that connected learning will happen in their classrooms (Beglau et al., 2011). A well respected, national meta-analysis about teaching and learning laments, "Many approaches to teaching adults consistently violate principles for optimizing learning" (Bransford, Brown, Cocking, Donovan, & Pellegrino, 2000, p. 26).

The Center for Public Education comments that 90 percent of teachers report participating in professional development, and most of these educators also believe that it was "totally useless" (Gulamhussein, 2013). That's because traditional professional development for teachers is frequently misaligned with best practices for connected learning. Instead, professional learning experiences are often top-down, autocratic, and didactic. The disjointed, one-shot workshop designs that typify professional development rarely generate desired changes. Research reveals that more than 14 aligned hours of professional development is required before student learning is affected and most teachers aren't receiving that level of support (Yoon, 2007).

If we're serious about creating schools that matter, then we must also get serious about creating effective learning experiences for teachers. Although this is a tall order, don't despair. The same tools that have accelerated the need for change also offer educators amazing new opportunities to "**power up**" professional learning in their schools and districts.

Often, these tools provide free ways of connecting people, practices, and ideas. They facilitate professional learning that is nimble, interactive, and effective.

SO, HOW CAN YOU GET STARTED?

The pages that follow provide you with one easy-to-implement, practical method for modeling a connected learning environment in your school, district, or region. Called Edcamp, the model leverages internal expertise, digital networks, and conversation to generate change. This book is the official "How to Edcamp" guide released by the Edcamp Foundation, a nonprofit, volunteer organization that supports Edcampers everywhere.

Edcamps are more than just an idea or theory; they're part of an international movement. The model has been replicated in 42 states and dozens of countries worldwide. Over 25,000 educators have participated in a regional Edcamp event, and many more have participated in an Edcamp-style event at their school. Thousands of blogs have been posted documenting both the Edcamp experience and concrete changes that teachers have made as a result of attending an Edcamp. An analysis of these reflections shows that Edcamps not only adhere to the tenets of effective adult learning, but they also prove highly motivating.

Get ready to meet Edcampers from every corner of the world, learn how to successfully organize an organic event with no predetermined schedule, and uncover ways to personalize professional learning for every teacher in your school, district, or region.

Edcamp is a proven model that you can use regardless of your specific situation. It typifies the organic, connected learning that is absolutely necessary in today's world.

Join the thousands of educators across the world who have "**powered up**" their professional learning with the Edcamp model. Read on.

Powering Up Professional Learning With the Edcamp Model

I learned more at Edcamp than I did at grad school. It was exactly the information I needed to know.

—*Karen Blumberg, teacher and technologist*

THE NEED FOR EDCAMPS

Traditionally, professional development for teachers has been isolated, passive, and top-down. Because of this poor design, many teachers dread traditional professional development days. Frequently termed "inservices," these learning events often lead to disengagement and boredom.

The prevalence of this predicament has led to a learning crisis for the adults leading our schools. According to a report released by the Center for American Progress, most teachers aren't engaging in enough professional learning to meet the ever-changing demands of the modern world (Gulamhussein, 2013). What this means is that in a society where being a good learner is tied to survival more than ever, the resources provided to teachers by their schools is not adequately keeping pace.

As our economy grows and changes, some refer to the growth of the *knowledge economy.* In the knowledge economy, jobs that require thinking, problem solving, and advanced education skills are valuable and available. Jobs that don't require academic and analytical skills are quickly becoming scarce, making the need to learn these proficiencies more important than ever.

To prepare students for the world of work (which will include many jobs that do not yet exist), teachers need to constantly refine and augment their practices. Teachers need time to learn from others, try out new strategies, and discuss the pressing issues of *now.* However, due to calendar constraints, shrinking budgets, and top-down mandates, many learning organizations simply don't have the resources to provide teachers with the professional development they need each day or each week.

Interestingly, the advent of the Internet has created an environment where content and connections are abundant. We can connect to others (and their ideas) more easily now than ever before. This creates a unique opportunity to learn in new, different ways that often transcend high price tags, traditional experts, or regional isolation. Many teachers all over the world are flocking to online spaces to "fill the gap" regarding their professional learning. For example, nightly synchronous chats on Twitter have sprung up all over the country. Teachers from near and far are engaging in conversations about design thinking, standards-based grading, project based learning, and more. However, there's more to connected learning than consumption. A critical component of connected learning requires one to share what they've learned with others (Swanson, 2012).

Just chatting and blogging online isn't enough. Research shows that teachers need physical communities of practice, extended discussion, and experimentation as they work through new strategies and modes of instruction (Beglau et al., 2011). Further, these communities must be local, face-to-face, and flexible, allowing teachers to respond to the most recent trends and areas of concern.

Enter Edcamp. Edcamp is a FREE form of professional development that allows teachers to become empowered, drive their own learning, and build face-to-face, personal communities of practice. It's easy to organize, even easier to attend, and locally sustainable. The format relies on the expertise of teachers and the power of interactive discussion.

The purpose of this book is to teach you how to run an Edcamp in your school, district, or region. It's a practical way to fight the professional development crisis that plagues many educators and school. Besides, it's also a lot of fun! The authors of this book, founders of the Edcamp model and educators themselves, believe that Edcamps allow schools, districts, and regions to better embark on their journey with connected learning. The format encourages educators to share and collaborate with their colleagues in ways that honor the expertise of each individual. As Edcamps are a proven model that's very easy to organize and implement, teachers or school leaders in virtually any organization can initiate them.

WHAT IS AN EDCAMP?

Edcamps are organic, participant-driven professional development experiences created by educators, for educators. All topics and discussions are generated collaboratively on the day of the event by all of the learners in attendance. Edcamps emphasize internal motivation, choice, and interactivity. Based on the tenets of open space technology, Edcamps are derived from the belief that a group of people, given a purpose and freedom, have the ability to self-organize, self-govern, and produce results (Boule, 2011). Conversations, not presentations, dominate the learning at an Edcamp. Every participant has an equal voice and personal expertise is honored.

The purpose of the Edcamp format is to empower all educators to honor their own expertise. The model is designed in a way that encourages peer learning, sharing, and collaboration. Educators who attend Edcamps have something of value to contribute. Working together, everyone advances the technique, pedagogy, and craft of the entire group.

WHAT MAKES AN EDCAMP UNIQUE?

Edcamps are unique because they are nimble, interactive, and social. Cutting-edge topics, active instructional designs, community cultivation, self-driven experiences, and long tail learning are a few of the features within each Edcamp that embody connected learning.

Cutting-edge, up-to-date topics

Since Edcamp schedules are created on the day of the event, they can always respond to the most needed, relevant topics for the group in attendance. This increases an Edcamp's ability to be oriented around personalized goals, one of the tenets of effective adult learning. Also, the access to the most current knowledge in context can increase participant's abilities to use what they've learned following the Edcamp event.

Instructional designs that rely on active learning

Edcamps are built around conversations and informal interactions. As lectures or rehearsed presentations are intentionally discouraged at an Edcamp, participants are required to interact and discuss during the day. This participatory format helps to move the learner beyond the mere acquisition of new content. It also gives many different voices the opportunity to share their learning. At traditional conferences or professional developments, only the "experts" are given time to present. At an Edcamp, everyone is viewed as an expert and all are granted the opportunity to present. This leveling of the playing field directly responds to societal shifts around the creation and distribution of new information and new knowledge. Adult learners should find purpose and relevance at an Edcamp event, two of the components that increase the transfer of learning into practice.

Vibrant communities of learners that go beyond school or district walls

Often, bringing different viewpoints together can result in innovation. Edcamps bring different educators from varied areas to collaborate and share, which, in turn, create vibrant connections and learning communities. In many cases, educators continue to connect in digital spaces long after the Edcamp event, continuing to create shared expertise on Twitter, blogs, and wikis. This aspect of Edcamps responds to the need for teacher professional development to be community-driven and social.

Self-driven

Educators choose the topics and information shared at an Edcamp. Learners are encouraged to craft their own itinerary and use the information in ways that make sense to them. This immense power is also accompanied by immense responsibility. When things go awry in an Edcamp experience, it's up to THE EDCAMPERS THEMSELVES to fix it. Some educators have quipped, "The only person to blame for a bad day at an Edcamp is *YOURSELF.*"

Long tail learning

Edcamp events have a long tail of learning because people make connections that continue long after the event is over. If you use Twitter as a backchannel during your event, participants can follow your event's hashtag for follow-up conversations and reflective blog posts. A backchannel is like a chat room where people publicly post resources and thoughts online. Some Edcamps have active hashtags year-round, with people sharing their thoughts and ideas among a common network of people who connected at a specific event.

TENETS OF THE EDCAMP MODEL

The following tenets define the Edcamp model.

EDCAMPS are:

- **free:** Edcamps should be free to all attendees. This helps ensure that all different types of teachers and educational stakeholders can attend.

- **noncommercial and with a vendor-free presence:** Edcamps should be about learning, not selling. Educators should feel free to express their ideas without being swayed or influenced by sales pitches for educational books or technology.

- **hosted by any organization or any one person:** Anyone should be able to host an Edcamp. School districts, educational stakeholders, and teams of teachers can host Edcamps.

- **composed of sessions that are determined on the day of the event:** Edcamps should not have prescheduled presentations. During the morning of the event, the schedule is created in conjunction with every current attendee. Sessions must be spontaneous, interactive, and responsive to participants' needs.

- **events where anyone who attends can be a presenter:** Anyone who attends an Edcamp is eligible to share or facilitate a session. All teachers and educational stakeholders are professionals worthy of sharing their expertise in a collaborative setting.

- **reliant on the law of two feet that encourages participants to find a session that meets their needs:** As anyone can host a session, it is critical that participants are encouraged to actively self-select the best content and sessions. Edcampers should leave sessions that do not meet their needs. This provides a uniquely effective way of "weeding out" sessions that are not based on appropriate research, or not delivered in an engaging format.

These tenets can serve as a roadmap toward connected learning and establishing an Edcamp at your school, district, or region.

EDCAMP PHILLY: A VIGNETTE

Despite the concrete definition, it can be difficult to truly capture the Edcamp experience. That's because a "typical" day of learning at an Edcamp doesn't really exist. Each Edcamp is unique and based on the needs of the participants.

So . . . what does an Edcamp actually look like? Here's a recap of last year's Edcamp Philly.

A planning team of 10 teachers began their work about three months before the event. Relying on donations from local universities, tech companies, and nearby restaurants, the team secured a venue and some breakfast goodies. Given that the team was operating on a shoestring budget, traditional advertising was not an option. Instead, Twitter, Facebook, word-of-mouth, and blogs were used to advertise the event. Within a few weeks, over 300 people had signed up to attend.

On the day of the event, dozens of educators arrived at the Philadelphia location. Signage consisted of printed papers and sidewalk chalk. A high school student created the event logo as part of his requirements for a drafting course. When everyone arrived, there was no pre-set schedule of sessions or presenters. Instead, there was just a blank sheet of big paper with a grid on it. The grid had spaces for participants to write in their session and conversation topics.

From that blank slate, everyone built the session schedule together. As people mingled and chatted over free coffee and donuts, they posted potential discussion topics on a board using colored paper. The entire process was positive and organic. Some people who didn't even know each other at the start of the day realized they had similar interests and ended up running a session together. Other folks arrived with an idea, threw it out to the group, revised it, and ended up posting it with a refined focus. Since anyone who attends an Edcamp event can be a session leader, it's a very empowering experience for everyone involved.

Once the schedule was built, it was time for the day to begin. To start, everyone gathered for a 15-minute kickoff from the organizers. This time was used to explain the expectation of discussion-based sessions and the rule of two feet. Next, folks wandered into the discussion rooms that most interested them. Several of the sessions focused on best practice, a few shared successful lessons, and others explored brand new protocols or tools. Social media outlets, such as Twitter and Google Docs, were used by many participants to share their learning and make lasting connections with other attendees. Throughout the day, folks followed "the rule of two feet" to make sure that the learning they experienced was interactive and relevant.

The end of the day was capped off with a session titled *Educational Smackdown* where folks could share their reflections or favorite takeaways from the camp.

Following the event, many attendees blogged about their learning and subsequent classroom implementations. Although not required, this step allowed the day to generate practical, long lasting effects on teacher practice.

This is just a single Edcamp story. There are hundreds of other Edcamp stories across the globe. In fact, there might be an Edcamp story happening in your town this week! Edcamp organizers have replicated this learning protocol in dozens of states and counties, empowering hundreds of thousands of teachers worldwide.

SO . . . HOW DO I ATTEND AN EDCAMP?

Is your interest peaked? Would you like to attend an Edcamp? Well, it's likely that there's already a regional Edcamp event planned near you. All Edcamp events are free to attend, and most Edcamp events happen on Saturdays to better accommodate your busy schedule. To see a complete listing of all Edcamp events (past, present, and future), go to http://Edcamp.wikispaces.com/complete+Edcamp+calendar. You can register for an upcoming event by going to the event's website and clicking on the ATTEND or REGISTER button.

If there are no Edcamps near you, then there are still other options. Some Edcamps, such as Edcamp Iowa, stream their entire day. This means that you can participate in the Edcamp right from the comfort of your own home! There are also virtual Edcamps, such as Edcamp Home and Edcamp Online. Again, all these Edcamps require to participate is an Internet connection.

Sometimes attending an Edcamp is the best way to truly learn about the model. As we know from our work with students, learning by doing works best. The best preparation for planning your own Edcamp is jumping in and attending one yourself!

Does Edcamp Really Work?

I had heard of Edcamps, but wondered if one day of conversation could have a REAL impact on me and my practice. I have been to Pro-D days where by 1 PM, I get a "I need a nap" attack and feel drained, checked out, and antsy by the end of the day.

This was different.

The day was full of light brightness and solidified my belief in the transformative power of connection.

—*Carolyn Durley, biology teacher*

Let's face it. Edcamps challenge most of what we accept as status quo in professional learning. You're likely wondering: Can FREE learning that's organized on the day of the event actually be any good?

WHAT EDUCATORS ARE SAYING ABOUT EDCAMP AND ITS EXPONENTIAL GROWTH

The verdict is in, and educators overwhelmingly support the Edcamp model. A whitepaper released in May 2012 by the Edcamp Foundation analyzed a series of random, spontaneous blog posts written by educators after experiencing an Edcamp. The most common emergent themes discussed by educators in the posts were

- the presence of effective collaboration at an Edcamp;
- the value of group expertise by creating the schedule together at an Edcamp;
- interactive instructional design through conversation at an Edcamp session;
- advanced knowledge of tech tools shared by colleagues at an Edcamp; and
- surprise at the dedication of other colleagues at an Edcamp.

Consider the following statements from educators around the globe:

"Not only is it respectful of our dedication to and knowledge about our craft, but it also holds us accountable to participate and lead. This is a powerful difference from most professional development sessions where teachers fight for the back row so they can grade papers without being seen while the presenter reads off the PowerPoint."

"Isn't this the true definition of collaboration? . . . Leaders who get this are not only better for it, but can lead others to create communities of excellence."

"It's not that all attendees all have the right answers, but Edcamp attendees still have a strong passion for this life that we've chosen and want so desperately to share it with other like-minded people."

Such positivity has spawned exponential growth of the movement since its inception in May of 2010. Over and over again, small groups of educators, both teachers and administrators, go outside the boundaries of standard professional development models and create their own Edcamp. The model is spreading like wildfire, appealing to thousands of educators who are willing to take time to learn and grow together.

As of February 2014, over 400 regional Edcamp events have been independently organized and held within 40 states and tens of countries. That doesn't even include the hundreds of Edcamp-style events held in schools and districts across the country each year! The consistent growth of the phenomenon is illustrated in the figure below.

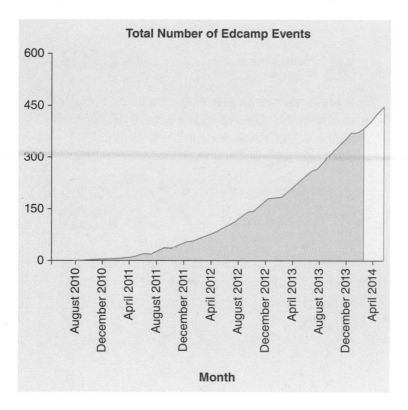

THE IMPACT ON STUDENT LEARNING

As Edcamps are organic and spontaneous, it can be hard to quantify the precise impact of an Edcamp event on student learning outcomes. Alas, this is a problem with studying many of the existing professional development models. In order to begin that study, we have started to chronicle the phenomenon and its effects.

Edcamps are highly regarded by the majority who participate. However, if Edcamps are to be considered truly successful, they must change teacher practice and classroom learning.

Social media and blogs are home to a growing body of evidence and teacher testimonials about how some practices have changed after an Edcamp event. Consider how these educators responded to the question: Has an Edcamp session significantly impacted your practice?

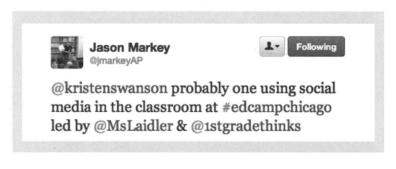

Jason Markey
@jmarkeyAP

@kristenswanson probably one using social media in the classroom at #edcampchicago led by @MsLaidler & @1stgradethinks

Daniel Scibienski
@danielscib

@kristenswanson 2 sessions stand out in my mind: in Philly, @mritzius on the integrated studies program & in NJ @paulbogush on body lang.

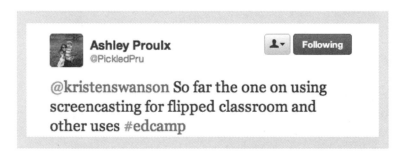

Ashley Proulx
@PickledPru

@kristenswanson So far the one on using screencasting for flipped classroom and other uses #edcamp

Joy Kirr
@JoyKirr

@kristenswanson One where we talked about all the cool things you could do with Evernote and how you can save everything there!

To be certain, the documentation of Edcamp's impact on student learning goes well beyond terse tweets. Consider the following three journeys from Edcampers across the globe and the specific ways that Edcamp transformed their classrooms.

EDCAMPER IN ACTION: CRAIG YEN

Craig Yen is an educator from California who recently joined the Edcamp movement. In a little under four months, he attended Edcamp SF Bay, Edcamp Sonoma, and Edcamp Los Altos.

Craig found the learning at the Edcamp events increasingly valuable, noting the following on his blog after Edcamp Los Altos: "I believe that it was on Friday that I registered for my next Edcamp. I think I'm addicted!"

Specifically, Craig learned about Mystery Skypes and the Global Read Aloud from his Edcamp experiences. After learning about these teaching strategies that encourage global collaboration in his classroom, Craig tried them out.

Again, Craig chronicled his learning on his blog. He writes:

Well our first one didn't quite go as expected. We had audio difficulties where the microphone in Google Hangout wasn't set up correctly on our classroom side. Talked over the phone to ask questions and the kids in the back channel did ask enough questions so that they were able to guess as well. Apologies and thanks to Todd Nesloney (@techninjatodd) and his class for putting up with us! :) Still there was a buzz before the call, during, and after asking when our next one would be.

I had set up three for the first round of mystery calls. The second one, we did yesterday with Elizabeth Willoughby's class. She worked away to go ahead and work out the kinks as at first, her video was locked so that she wasn't sending a video through Google Hangouts. She had previously only used Skype. What was interesting with her class was that her class used sports questions to try to narrow down our location.

We had some good questions from our side, for instance, "Are you landlocked?" This made the kids think more about the different regions and geographical terms continuing to allow them to think.

For the next call I want to float more around the room to see what is going on at the other jobs . . . Our audio with speakers left a little to be desired. Perhaps an audio extension cord. Overall, a success though.

It's clear that Craig's Edcamp learnings are having a practical impact on his classroom. Edcamps are connecting Craig to new ideas and new colleagues all over the United States. Because of Edcamp, Craig's 5th graders have engaged in more collaboration and more critical thinking.

EDCAMPER IN ACTION: SEAN WHEELER

Sean Wheeler is a teacher at Lakewood City High School in Ohio. Sean was a bit skeptical of the Edcamp model at first. However, he was eventually persuaded to attend Edcamp Columbus by one of his colleagues.

When Sean attended his first Edcamp, he was about to embark on a design-centered unit with his students. To his delight, a session on design was offered by his fellow colleagues.

Sean writes on his blog about how the Edcamp session influenced his design-centered unit and ultimately impacted his students. He writes:

> Design interests me a great deal, and it was great to see a session offered on Human Centered Design. It was a powerful session and I think the conversation will have an impact on my work for a while. I'm in the planning stages of doing some really cool research with my students, and it helped to be refocused on the vital concept that students need to be central while designing the work for the upcoming project. Sometimes I get lost in how I would teach something instead of how students might want to learn it.

Sean's instructional unit is forever changed by the conversations he had with colleagues specifically tailored to his interests and needs.

EDCAMPER IN ACTION: HEIDI SWIAK

Heidi Swiak is a teacher in Ontario who attended and organized both Edcamp Toronto and Edcamp Hamilton. Both Edcamps left such an impression on Heidi that she decided to begin an Inquiry Working Group.

She writes:

> What I wanted was a working group—people passionate and dedicated to learning more about inquiry who want to meet regularly to share and learn. I wanted the value of the Edcamp model, but I wanted more than just one day. So I created the Inquiry Working Group and invited others to join me on a new journey.

And so, Heidi invited 15 colleagues to join her on an extended learning journey. At the first meeting, Heidi found a specific strategy from a colleague that impacted her practice.

Heidi shares:

> My change in practice take away came from Tonya. When she is conducting large class lessons, students are free to

write their questions on sticky notes—many of us do this. Tonya's twist, however, is the Question Board. All questions are posted on the board and discussed. Students who are intrigued by other students' questions are free to take them and explore them more deeply. Clever!

Not only did Heidi have a great learning experience at her Edcamp events, but they also spurred a long-standing connection to her colleagues that directly impacted student learning.

While there are still many opportunities to research the impact of connected learning and the Edcamp model on student outcomes, the evidence collected to date indicates that observable change is happening worldwide.

EDCAMPER IN ACTION: LAKSMI PUSPITOWARDHANI

Laksmi is a teacher in Indonesia who organized the first Edcamp event in her country. Despite the fact that many teachers in her area were very skeptical of the model before attending, she ended up having an extremely successful event. The global networking that she did to organize the event inspired her to bring similar experiences to her students.

She writes:

At this point, as a homeroom teacher in primary school, the collaboration was inspiring me to bring the same thing to my classroom. I want to give my students the opportunity to feel the experience working with the students from the other part of the world, having their own wow experience. Now, I'm looking forward to have global class collaboration. EXCITED!

Not only did Laksmi organize a groundbreaking event in her country, but the act of putting together the learning experience influenced the ways she considered how she taught kids.

THE "YES, BUTS . . ."

As you reach this section of the text, it's likely you still have some questions about the viability of the Edcamp model. That's completely normal. In fact, the Edcamp Foundation fields hundreds of "yes, but" questions each month in an effort to educate people and build their confidence as they organize their first event. Read on for answers to some of the most frequently asked questions facing new Edcamp organizers.

Yes, but . . . what if no one puts anything on the schedule board?

It's likely that for all first-time organizers there will be considerable anxiety about the schedule-building process on the day of the event. While fear is natural when trying something new, don't let this discomfort paralyze the day. There have been hundreds of successful Edcamps to date, all with filled session boards. In fact, there has never been an Edcamp where everyone showed up, but no one was willing to present. That's part of the magic!

However, it's important to recognize that any Edcamp-style professional development you organize at your own school site might present unique challenges. This is usually because individuals may be hesitant to volunteer in front of the colleagues with whom they work every day. Lessen this discomfort by beginning the day with a whole-group brainstorm session or offering discussion table topics. If you know a colleague that has something to share, encourage them to run a session. In the beginning the organizers may need to suggest particular sessions or partner individuals to run a session together.

Also, don't forget to include everyone in your day of learning, including your administrators. Small sessions run by administrators, whether they be purely instructional or discussion-based sessions, are often very popular. The goal is to have administration embrace and model participatory learning.

Yes, but . . . what if someone shares something that is wrong?

Edcamps honor the expertise of educators. However, that does not imply that every educator is an expert at everything. There may be times when someone shares something that's incorrect or biased. However, if you're a connected educator you have access to a wealth of information at your fingertips. Most commonly, when someone shares erroneous information at an Edcamp, others speak up to challenge the idea. If divergent viewpoints are not accepted in a session, it's common for Edcampers to leave the session via the rule of two feet; this method ensures that accuracy is honored.

Yes, but . . . what if someone just presents a PowerPoint?

Despite your best efforts to communicate the conversational nature of Edcamp sessions, you may have a presenter who simply reads through PowerPoint slides. Often, Edcampers will leave the session when this happens via the Rule of Two Feet. It's impossible to flawlessly police the content at an Edcamp. However, reinforcing the Rule of Two Feet and setting expectations for the day can minimize ineffective learning situations.

Yes, but . . . is this model sustainable?

As with any innovation, it's important to discuss the sustainability. Can educators from around the globe continue to offer free, organic learning experiences year after year? Will Edcamp organizers continue to find value in giving of their time and talents over and over again?

A close examination of the initial data set reveals that the model is capable of sustaining itself.

From 2010 to 2012, 184 regional Edcamp events were held all over the world. Of these 184 events, only 28 events did not have a follow-up event. More specifically, only 15 percent of all the events held between 2010 and 2012 did not go on to become a semiannual, biannual, or annual event.

Importantly, many of the events that continue year after year (e.g., Edcamp Detroit, Edcamp NYC, Edcamp Harrisburg, etc.) have increased in size and available resources. These events have become local fixtures in the educational communities. The number of participants in the Edcamp model continues to grow, and over 25,000 educators have participated in an Edcamp to date.

The Edcamp model is sustainable, and the community fostered through Edcamp events can persist over time. The data shows that it's not a passing fad. Educators teaching educators never goes out of style.

WE'RE STILL LEARNING

As with any new innovation, there is always more to learn. Edcampers across the globe and the Edcamp Foundation continue to study the Edcamp model and its effects. More work is needed to measure the impact of this model on student learning outcomes. As the number of Edcamp events continues to increase, the Edcamp Foundation continues to collaborate with organizers and document the experiences. Visit www.edcamp.org for more information.

Organizing an Edcamp-Style Event at Your School or District

Edcamp changed my life. Happy to help. Rock on.

—*Daniel Scibienski, English*
Language Learner consultant

BRING THE BENEFITS OF AN EDCAMP-STYLE PROFESSIONAL DEVELOPMENT TO YOUR SCHOOL OR DISTRICT

Bringing Edcamp-style professional development to your school or district is an exciting proposition. Not only does it increase the amount of personalized, connected learning available to your staff, but it also generates effective professional development opportunities without the cost of bringing in an expensive presenter.

BEFORE YOU START: CONNECTING TO THE EDCAMP COMMUNITY

The Edcamp Community is a vibrant collection of educators from across the globe. Edcampers are helpful, connected individuals who delight in learning and sharing. Before you start planning your learning event, take the time to visit the resources below and connect with other Edcampers near you. They'll become an invaluable resource to you as you move forward with the process.

- **The Edcamp Wiki**—http://edcamp.wikispaces.com—This is the official Edcamp wiki maintained by the Edcamp Foundation. It has a complete listing of all upcoming Edcamp events, logo files you can edit, helpful videos, and landing pages for all Edcamp events. Join the wiki and begin contributing!
- **The Edcamp Foundation Site**—http://www.edcamp.org— This site is the homepage of the Edcamp Foundation. Here you can learn more about programs to help Edcamp organizers, current sponsors, and cutting-edge information about the Edcamp movement.
- **The Edcamp Foundation Partner Program**—http://edcamp .org/mini-grants/—Here you can apply to receive assistance from the Edcamp Foundation Partner Program. In this program, you are paired with an experienced Edcamp organizer who answers questions and directs you to resources. It's a great way to get your event off the ground!
- **The Edcamp Foundation Whitepaper**—http://edcamp .org/2012/07/edcamp-a-qualitative-exploration-whitepaper/— At this site, you can download research on the Edcamp movement, including links to best practices for adult learning.

- **The Edcamp Hashtag on Twitter**—https://twitter.com/search? q=%23Edcamp&src=typd—This Twitter site shows you real-time conversations around the world about the Edcamp movement.
- **Edcamp Example for Schools**—Joe Mazza runs an Edcamp-style event at his school: *http://efacetoday.blogspot.com/ 2012/08/Edcamp-comes-to-knapp-elementary-part-1.html*
- **Edcamp Example for Districts**—Patrick Larkin creates an Edcamp-style event at his district: *http://bpscon.org/*

GETTING STARTED

Now that you've learned about the origins of Edcamp as well as the research behind the model, you are fully prepared to host your own Edcamp event at your school. As district or school professional learning events are generally mandatory for all faculty members and not open to everyone, in-house events are often described as "Edcamp-style" events.

Veteran Edcamp organizers may tell you the only things you need are (1) a date, and (2) a venue. However, logistics are only one piece of the puzzle; assessing the culture of your learning organization is actually the first step.

CONSIDERING CULTURE

Every organization has a unique culture, and this must be considered before organizing an Edcamp-style professional development day. If your school's culture is positive, forward-thinking, and collaborative, your organization is primed for an Edcamp-style event. If, on the other hand, your school's culture includes traditionalism and isolationism, for the event to be successful, you will need to educate participants. Lean in with the full knowledge that many others have brought connected professional learning to their schools with great success. Model the enthusiasm you hope to generate and be patient, if necessary.

For example, don't get discouraged if it takes a little time to generate enthusiasm for the Edcamp model within your school system. Peter DeWitt, an Edcamper from northern New York, wasn't able to generate enough interest for his in-house, districtwide, Edcamp-style event the first time he tried. Sharing his experience in a recent *Education Week* article, he cites the following factors as things to consider when organizing an in-house event:

- Timing—Peter started the Edcamp campaign at the end of September/early October which was the same time that teachers finished completing their first ever state-mandated curriculum assessment. Teachers indicated that they didn't have time to consider attending and presenting.

- Accountability, New Initiatives, and Burnout—For Peter, because of the accountability they were all under, that school year had been like no other. Teachers inside the district felt stifled and overwhelmed by new initiatives.

- Lack of the Power of Connecting—One of the reasons why Edcamps are trending ideas around the country is because they are being done at a state or regional level, not necessarily a district-level. Social media plays a huge part in it because most of the attendees and all of the presenters are on Twitter and the excitement builds naturally over months through those online conversations. Before you organize the event, it is very helpful if you make sure that people see the value in connecting with their colleagues.

Be thoughtful and empathetic when designing your first in-house event. What are people thinking and feeling? What is the best way to meet people "where they are"? Putting yourself in someone else's shoes can often help you achieve success.

CONVINCING SCHOOL LEADERS WHO ARE SKEPTICAL OF OPEN LEARNING

Most often, school leaders who resist the idea of an Edcamp-style event do so because they believe that the need for mandated instruction is too great to allocate time for open, participant-driven learning. Also, some school leaders wonder whether time that isn't planned will be valuable. Fear of losing control can exist for school leaders. However, compromise is the key to success with Edcamp-style events. Many hybrid in-house events have been run that value the needs of every stakeholder.

When dealing with the need for mandated instruction, there are several ways to integrate these sessions with sessions of the participant's choosing. Infusing organic sessions often serves to soften the dictated feeling of in-house professional development. For example, you can offer the mandatory sessions at several times during the day. Some individuals choose to attend mandatory sessions early in the day, others may opt for a session directly after lunch or at the end of the day. Empowering faculty with a few options communicates a great respect for their time, professionalism, and accountability to their own learning. Another way to integrate mandatory sessions is to flip them, recording them for viewing either during the professional development or at another time of the staff's choosing.

Regarding the fear that unplanned time won't be productive, it can often be helpful to share stories from leaders who have embraced the Edcamp model. Administrators, such as Patrick Larkin, assistant school superintendent, Joe Mazza, connected teacher and leader, and Tom Murray, research scholar have all run successful Edcamp-style events in their schools. All of them report that the time was very fruitful and closely linked to organization-level student learning goals. Archives of their experiences exist on their blogs, and these can be powerful artifacts when showing an administrator the value of the Edcamp model. Be sure to check out Joe's popular post entitled "Edcamp Comes to Knapp Elementary" here: http://www.leadlearner.com/Edcamp-comes-to-knapp-elementary-part-1/.

As mentioned earlier, Edcamps are only one part of an effective program for professional development and Edcamp-style, in-house professional development will likely not meet all educators' needs at all times. However, administrators that embrace participant-driven learning as a significant piece of teacher learning send a clear message that they value the expertise within their school walls. Something as simple as an Edcamp-style event can enhance a school's culture and invigorate faculty.

SETTING THE STAGE FOR SUCCESS

Generate positive momentum by educating your colleagues about the tenets of Edcamp (see Chapter 1). People may not be familiar with the format, and it's critical to manage expectations leading up to your event. Sharing blog posts, videos, and articles about Edcamp works well. Importantly, send clear messages about not only how the schedule is built (together on the morning of the event), but also about the kinds of sessions that are an ideal match for Edcamp. Most Edcamp sessions fall into one of three areas:

- **Passions**—Those things they have a lot of experience with, absolutely love, and want to share with as many people as possible. *I am a strong believer in Universal Design for Learning, and can't wait to share everything I know about it with the people at Edcamp.*

- **Interests**—Areas they are somewhat familiar with, but would love an opportunity to get together with others and extend their own thinking. *I've started using iPads in my classroom and think they could be very powerful for student learning. I think we could get a group of people together to share all of our ideas for using them in school.*

- **Questions**—Bodies of knowledge that they know almost nothing about, but know they want to learn about from people with experience. *I'm a preservice teacher and I know that assessment is very important to running a good classroom. I wonder what some of the best assessment strategies are?*

The instructional design of each session is also really important. You need to repeatedly reinforce that Edcamp sessions are *highly interactive*. If one or two people are talking in front of a room for the entire time, that's a poorly designed session for an Edcamp, even if it would be a *great* presentation at a traditional conference. Sessions can address any educational topic of interest. At an Edcamp, everybody should be participating in the sessions, either because they're strongly conversation-based or a hands-on examiner of tools and ideas. Examples of well-received Edcamp sessions include:

- **Things That Suck**—This is a conversation-based format where controversial topics (letter grades, homework, Internet filters) are thrown to the room and people move to different sides based on their own positive (rocks) or negative (sucks) experiences with it. The two sides then rapidly share their experiences for a brief period of time (7 minutes). Despite its flippant title, the session is a positive format where people can openly debate best practice. This session is fun, fast-paced, and filled with opportunities to see how things work in other schools.

- **Introduction to Twitter**—Many teachers coming to your Edcamp will be new to ideas about Connected Learning. A hands-on session where they get set up with an account and learn the basics of tweeting helps them understand the power of Twitter.

- **Student Panels**—Sometimes, students attend an Edcamp with their teachers. A panel format where the students share their own experiences in the classroom, but the questions all come from the educators in the room is a powerful opportunity to see things from the other side of the desk.

- **Guided Inquiry Protocol**—The facilitator for this session outlines a clear goal for the session (i.e., explore the role of assessment in a Project Based Learning unit). From there, the facilitator asks three to five questions that directly guide participants toward the crux of the issue. Questions are shared at the beginning of the session.

- **The Smackdown**—These are held as a whole-group activity to end the day at many Edcamps; this is a fast-paced opportunity for people to share with the whole group one of their favorite tools, books, teaching strategies, or resources in two minutes or less.

If you've done your job well and made people comfortable with the way sessions are formulated and designed, then you're going to get to witness one of the most impactful things you've ever experienced as an educator: seeing a group of committed professionals take a completely blank schedule board and fill it up with an amazing roster of activities and conversations so that there's a wide variety of sessions that meet the needs of everybody in the room.

THE DAY OF YOUR EVENT: A STEP-BY-STEP GUIDE

Step 1: Prepare Your Venue

You will probably elect to hold your Edcamp event in your school or at another school in your area. Just make sure you have the following spaces and resources available:

1. A main auditorium or gathering space capable of holding all attendees at once

2. Rooms for small groups to gather and have discussions (typically, one discussion room per every 25 Edcampers in attendance)

3. Free wireless Internet

4. Plenty of free nearby parking

5. Coffee, lots of coffee

Step 2: Build the Schedule

For many, building the schedule is the most ambiguous part of the Edcamp process. While there are certainly no "wrong" ways to build an Edcamp schedule, the tips below can set you up for success.

To begin, hang a large piece of poster paper in a prominent gathering place (preferably near the coffee!). Create a grid of session times and room numbers. Provide markers and Post-its nearby so that people can post their session ideas on the board.

Here is a sample blank schedule board:

People should come up to the board, put a topic and their name on a post-it, and stick it on the board. Once an idea is posted to the board, your Edcamp event has a session of learning!

At first, you may need to encourage people to sign up, but once a few sessions are posted, it is common for other people to quickly follow suit. Sometimes, people propose similar session topics. In these cases, you can encourage people to "combine forces" to make the learning even more collaborative. Having coffee and breakfast goodies available during this time can make the process feel more casual and collaborative. Also, have organizers walking through the crowd or venue to welcome everyone to the event. Making everyone feel comfortable goes a long way during the schedule-building portion of the day.

Here are some sample sessions from Edcamps worldwide:

- *Engagement, Respect, and Reciprocity in Public/Private School Partnerships* by Chris Thinnes at Edcamp LA 2013(@curtisCFEE)
- *We Taught 6th Graders Quantum Physics with Dance* by Miller Rothlein at Edcamp Philly 2012 (@MiroDance)
- *How to Address Privacy and One's Digital DNA* by Nancy Sharoff and Beth Knittle at Edcamp Boston 2012 (@nsharoff and @bknittle)

- *Design Thinking and Innovation* by Don Buckley at Edcamp New York City 2012

- *Writing in the Digital Age* by Toshi Carleton at Edcamp Leadership British Columbia 2012

The goal of the schedule-building process is to give every person in attendance at the Edcamp event the ability to shape the learning that happens over the course of the day. Providing unrestricted access to the schedule board fosters the type of professional empowerment that can bridge the gap between what schools can "provide" and what teachers can sustainably learn from each other.

As you encourage folks to post sessions to the board, remember to tell them that you can post topics that you'd like to share OR learn about. You don't need to be an expert on a topic to run a session. In fact, some of the best sessions are those where you can get feedback and resources from your peers on something that interests you.

Some events use voting to determine which sessions actually appear on the session board. Unless you have an experienced group of Edcampers, this strategy can be detrimental to the process. If folks know that the event they proposed could be "voted down," then they may be less likely to post something on the session board. Posting all proposed sessions and combining sessions where overlap exists is the best way to build a schedule, especially if it's your first time running an Edcamp event.

Many Edcamps also create a digital version of the schedule board so that people can check the schedule from their mobile devices and laptops throughout the day. Google Docs have proved to be the most popular, free tool for this purpose.

Here are some sample session boards from Edcamps:

Edcamp New York:

	Library	Rm. 404C	Rm. 404D	Rm. 405A	Rm. 405B	Rm. 406A	Rm. 406B
10.00 – 11.00	Apps Script Systems Revolution – How lo-fi tools, built by educators, are transforming the classroom, school, and district – Andrew Stillman @astillman	iTunes U - @earizzo57	Creation and digital management of student assessments, assessment data and grades in the elementary school tech lab	The Future of Textbooks, iBooks, and Tablets	Augmented Reality in k – 12 Education Courtney Pere - @ipadqueen2012	Common Core Math/ Tech! @RossCoops31	Tom Whitby PLN
11.20 – 12.20	Expand Everything! iPad and Android screencasting! Let's Get Creative @reshanrichman	Introduction to Schoology … Why using an LMS makes sense – Phil Cook @cookp	Taking control of Your PD: The What, The How, The Why – Ross LeBron	Music Making 4 All with the iPad – Adam Goldberg	Skype in the Classroom – who, why, how - @KatyGartside	Integration: Moving Past STEAM (and 8 other acronyms) – Jay Heath @heathjw	QLOVI – Imagine Literacy: EdTech* LMS* Assessment* Reading* Writing* K-students achieve literacy (and love to read)?
12.40 – 1.40	Out of Your Seat and On Your Feet	Crowd Teaching: The Crowd vs. Khan Academy @socraticorg	Global Collaboration on the iPad – Meg Wilson @iPodsibilities	The Future of Libraries … (have you done something interesting with your library? Want to?) – Emily Graves @msgraves214	Intro to Edmodo	Getting STEAMy Hands On Rube Goldbergs that bridge physical and digital worlds – Jaymes Dee, Dylan Ryder	Assistive Technology in a Life Skills Classroom

All Sessions are on the 4th Floor.

Follow the #edcampnyc tweets here: http://tagboard.com/edcampnyc

Edcamp Boston:

Floor	4th	4th	4th	2nd	2nd
Room:	Longfellow	Hawthorne	Thoreau	Concord	Bunker Hill
capacity:	60	60	40	40	25
8:15-9:30	Registration, Breakfast, Schedule Creation on 4th Floor				
9:30-10:20 Session #1	Using Tools to support collaboration. Evemote, Typelink, Carbon Fin @whsrowe	Game On! Game-Based Learning in (and out of) the classroom	Sharing strategies to get kids GLOBALLY connected	Do TOO Many kids go to college? A debate @courtney_nemett	Crowdsourcing the creation of a perfect school and How to Use ideas in your class. @mytakeonit
10:30-11:20 Session #2	Talk with REAL 5th Graders about 1:1 iPads! @dancallahan @idelia	Help!! Must learn MINECRAFT	I Believe WHAT I SEE Power of Visualization in science & Math @rbandekar	Using Socrative to check for Understanding @PMMSSS Patrick Morrissey	Getting Faulty to Innovate (How do we reach every teacher?) @whsrave @edtech2innovate
11:30-12:20 Session #3	iPad Pilot one year later . . . @lizbdavis	W.O.W. "Worthy of the world" Elementary Tech/Library Projects	The direction of science educational Group forum/ conversation @mrmusseiman	Mobile & Formative Assessment @shawnCRubin	APPRENTICE LEARNING: How 8th graders got jobs using iPads Helen Russen and Jeremy Angoff
12:30-12:55 Demo time	LUNCH!	LUNCH!	LUNCH!	Stem connecting science & math to the real world	Metryx Mobile Formative Assessment @shawnCRubin @MyMetryx
1:30-2:20 Session #4	Edcamp in the classroom @KatrinaKennett @beerogerz	Math middle/ upper @ fabmathtutor	Rent-a-Librarian Build a better research/inquiry project w/ research expert!! @idelia	A student's perspective: tech tools for struggling learners Sam Mahler Karen Janowski @karenjan @samson548 (9th grader)	BYOT/BYOD Why, @mytakeonit (Jeremy Angoff) #BYOTchat
2:30-3:20 Session #5	Defining the vision of what students today should know @lizbdavis http://bit.ly/ edcampvision		How do we balance creativity AND standards? @sguditus	How to get kids to ask questions in K–2 @ mgohagon@juss	TPACK & SAMR
3:30-4:30	Smackdown!				
5:00 -?	Afterparty at Meadhall – 4 Cambridge Center, Cambridge, MA				

2nd	2nd	2nd	2nd	2nd
Constitution	Lexington	Mayflower	Reception Lounge (no projector)	Breakout Table (no projector)
10	10	8	10	5
Blogging in the HS classroom @runningdoc	App Smashing 4 workflow @kidwellp	K–2 Computational Thinking: What is it? What does it look like?	Ed Eval in the Cloud. What are you doing?	Apps for Art and Photo
How to teach students to LISTEN http://bit.ly/edcamp	Stealing moments of calm in the chaos (Tai Chi Chin)	The new Mass Educator Evaluation for air) @Sguditus	Becoming Badass -> How do teachers get/stay brave.	
Using SCHOOLOLOGY to collaboratively create a US History course. @thalesdream	Apps promoting social development @speechtechie @sipmeg @shevtech	Using Tech for PBL—Are you up to the challenge? Problem Based Learning	What's working for Professional Development	
Learnist (curation/social learning) @runningdme		Digital Storytelling @30hands	Librarian's lunch	
How do I teach 21st century skills w/out 21st century resources?	Google + for PD @jmpcronin @pamelapiperach	Ebooks and Comprehension Apps @shawncrubin	Moving "Beyond Books" – How important (or not) are print resources? What would a school library look like? @ ellenbrandt	How do I HELP teach 21st century kids w/o 21st century resources?
How do we reach EVERY student? Discussion @karenjan	Using Chrome Books with your students? Share ideas! @gonfitz	3D Printing in the classroom	Coteaching Successes & setbacks @mshoreik	Supporting ELLs in the Content Class

As you can see from the examples above, most sessions are about one hour in length. However, you are encouraged to vary the layout and format of your day to best meet the needs of the group. Also, note that the topics are very diverse and varied between events. That's completely normal because the people in the room likely have interests that reflect their unique individuality.

Finally, Edcamp sessions can be about ANY topic. Because past Edcamp events have attracted a large majority of tech-savvy educators, there were many Edcamp sessions that addressed instructional technology topics. However, an Edcamp is not a technology experience, it's a *learning* experience. Sessions can really cover any topic of interest to the people in the room. Making this fact well-known during the schedule building process can allay any fears that less tech-savvy educators may have.

Once your schedule is built, you're ready to begin the day.

Step 3: Kick Off Your Event

Before you release everybody to their sessions, hold a brief kick-off to set the tone for the day. Begin by reminding everyone of Edcamp's tenets. Be sure to emphasize the most important thing participants need to know in order to make the day successful for themselves: The Rule of Two Feet. Unlike traditional professional development, everybody at Edcamp is encouraged to leave a session that's not meeting their needs at any time. There could be any number of reasons: the session wasn't what they expected, the level of conversation was not appropriate to their current needs, or even, unfortunately, that the session was poorly designed. Make sure that everyone clearly understands that walking out of the room is *not* an insult to the facilitator or other participants in the room. On the contrary, it's a commitment by everyone in attendance that they'll maximize every second of learning time.

You should also remind everyone in attendance about Wifi passwords, how to access the virtual schedule board, and lunch logistics. These small reminders help everyone feel comfortable, making your day a success!

Step 4: Facilitate Participant-Driven Sessions

Throughout the day, enjoy the organic learning that happens among colleagues. Organizers of successful Edcamp events recommend the following strategies to keep your Edcamp on track:

- **Float between sessions throughout the day.** Not only does this give you a better understanding of how your event is going, but it also gives session leaders the ability to ask for help if needed.

- **Keep an eye out for people who look lost.** Some may find the event overwhelming. Try to welcome them and connect them with others.

- **Have someone man the schedule board.** It's very common for Edcampers to add additional sessions to the session board after the day has started. Having someone available at the paper session board to answer questions and make adjustments is very helpful!

Step 5: Close Your Event

At the end of the Edcamp day, it's traditional to include a brief opportunity for all participants to share what they've learned. Many Edcamps end the day with a session called a "smackdown" where participants take turns quickly (usually two minutes each) sharing learnings, resources, tools, and tips. Individuals volunteer to come to a computer that is linked to a screen, and they discuss their learning or resource. As each person shares, a volunteer creates a document to capture the shared knowledge and makes it publicly available to the entire group. It's also common at the end of the day to ask attendees to fill out an evaluation of the event. Edcamp STL (St. Louis) is one example of this. Here are the questions and results from their 2013 event.

During the event there were:

307 teachers registered

215 showed up the day of the event

1593 tweets were sent out by participants

90 people completed the survey

Where did you hear about Edcamp STL?

39% Twitter

50% friend or colleague

0% Google Plus

2% Facebook

1% from their administrators

What did you think of the physical location? 1 = low, 5 = awesome

3—6%

4—21%

5—66%

What did you think of the date of the event? 1 = low, 5 = awesome

3—18%

4—22%

5—70%

How would you rate the food? 1 = yikes, 5 = awesome

1—4%

2—8%

3—32%

4—26%

5—26%

What did you think of the prizes? 1 = low, 5 = awesome

4—27%

5—62%

Favorite part of the day:

- The quick conversations about something new

- Networking

- The making place

- Sessions 3 and 4, I did "Getting Kids Moving" and "Differentiation"

- The maker room was amazing

- The discussions all throughout

- All of it, but it wouldn't have been the same without the free time (lunch and break times) to connect personally in informal conversations!

- The hallway conversations

- Being able to talk with other educators during lunch

- Ukulele class

- Networking

- Spending time with and learning from awesome educators!

- The no-cost fee!

- Getting to converse and share ideas and make connections

- with people throughout the educational field

- The sessions

- Talking!!!

- Connecting with so many people

- Discussing with others

- Space and time to process

- Learning with a bunch of caring, innovative, passionate educators from different levels, positions, and from all over the country. Very inspirational!

- The Google Chrome presentation was the highlight for me

- Prizes!

- Makerspace

- The whole day . . . this was my first Edcamp experience. . . . really great experience!!

- The presentations were great and I learned soooooo much. Loved Loved Loved making my pin at Maker Space!

(Continued)

- My third session—we had a fantastic discussion about the trend of education. It was back and forth and input from all parts of the room.
- Being able to choose
- Break outs
- Hard to say. Almost all of my sessions were good.
- My favorite part of the day was the opportunity to talk with other teachers.
- The learning in sessions—hearing what other teachers do and use
- Talking with other teachers
- The conversation
- Sharing and learning new ideas
- Sessions and networking. Conversations outside of sessions— it's all good
- Evernote session and all of the ideas that accompanied it really impressed me.
- I left Edcamp proud that there are so many quality educators in our region. Very refreshing.
- The sessions were great and quite varied
- The make it station

- Networking, extending learning in the halls and at lunch
- Teachers talking about integration. From the ground
- Hanging out with the robot people & kids in that room. Learning something new (making the light-button)
- Listening to the things other educators are doing in their classrooms
- The session about Nearpod, facilitating a discussion and networking!
- The sessions. This year it was the Ukulele session!
- Enjoyed making the pins, Friday evening, enjoyed the standardized grading class, prizes
- Being able to brainstorm with my peers! Did not like sessions with a "presenter"; not collaborative which is what I was expecting.
- I loved working with the robots. Your after-lunch activity was fun
- Meeting other educators in a comfortable and relaxed atmosphere

- Learning about the Photo computer class was helpful for me
- After lunch activity
- The whole day was fine
- Relaxed yet informative
- It was all great!
- 1st session–nearpod
- The sessions and discussion are always the best part
- I truly believe you learn things at Edcamp that can be implemented almost immediately if you really wanted to
- I have been both years now and feel like it is always a great day that is well spent
- I really enjoyed the meeting rooms, hearing from so many teachers it was very exciting!
- Networking, meeting new people between sessions. Not to take away from the sessions, they sparked more conversations.
- Getting to choose what sessions to go to and the casual atmosphere. The sessions. Networking and talking is great, but I came for

the sessions. I think the planning committee did an excellent job and being my first time, I will definitely return and recruit more to come with me next time. Thank you for putting in the work.

- Selecting from a wide variety of topics being presented and networking
- The break out session that talked about new trends in education. Very powerful!
- Makerspace!
- Learning and collaborating
- Collaborating, sharing and brainstorming with other educators
- Listening to other people share
- Listening to a kindergarten teacher discuss class management
- Conversations with new friends!
- Learning about Evernote
- Networking with people, maybe more time between sessions to share & reflect
- Lunch activity

Step 6: Reflect on and Refine Your Event

After your event is over, take time with your colleagues to discuss what went well and what could have gone better. If you asked participants to fill out a feedback form, discuss those results as well. Practically, make a list while it's still fresh in your collective memory because details will fade quickly. Were the conversations truly authentic or were they more like "presentations"? Did everything go well with the facility? The schedule? Were some sessions overloaded while others were nearly empty? Consider writing up a blog post or staff newsletter recapping things worth sharing with a wide audience.

INSET: A HELPFUL CHECKLIST FOR THE DAY OF YOUR EVENT

"DAY OF" EDCAMP EVENT CHECKLIST

Upon Arrival

- Divide up the various tasks for the event among your team. These can include:
  - Serving as greeters at the door
  - Managing a sign-in table
  - Hanging signage
  - Keeping track of the schedule board
  - Serving breakfast and coffee

Setting Up the Venue

- Someone should take the lead on managing the event space. Tasks include:
  - Preparing microphones, projectors, or other audiovisual needs for the kickoff/closure space
  - Preparing speakers and projectors in all meeting rooms
  - Ensuring all furniture can be easily moved to accommodate flexible conversations
  - Checking that the WIFI is working and available to all participants

Building the Schedule Board

- Appoint one person to manage the schedule board. Tasks include:
  - Hanging the large paper schedule board
  - Encouraging people to sign up for a session
  - Recording every session onto a virtual document so people can view the schedule from their devices throughout the day

Kicking Off the Event

- Determine who is leading the event kickoff. Remarks should include:
  - Tenets of Edcamp, especially the Rule of Two Feet
  - Thank you to attendees and sponsors
  - Logistical reminders about the length of each session and lunch

Event Closure

- Ensure the close of the day goes positively and smoothly. Do the following:
  - Develop an organized way (raffle tickets, calling by name, etc.) of distributing giveaways to attendees if necessary
  - Collect data about participants' experiences via an online survey

Tips for Running a Regional Edcamp Event

What makes EdCamp stand apart from other professional-development opportunities is teachers choose to come there on their own on a Saturday, so right there the commitment level is different. They're there to share and to learn. That collaborative spirit of the conference really makes it stand apart from anything else I've ever attended.

—*Meeno Rami, Educator, Author*

At the time this text was written, there had been over 400 regional Edcamp events worldwide. Regional Edcamp events are open to anyone, and they can be run by anyone.

Regional Edcamp events are typically held on Saturdays to accommodate educators' schedules. Begin by checking out the Complete Edcamp Calendar at http://Edcamp.wikispaces.com/complete+Edcamp+calendar on the official Edcamp Wiki site.

Here, you can find out if any regional Edcamps are being held in your area. It's possible that there may be one happening nearby! You may be able to learn from other Edcamp organizers in your area or possibly even join forces (if your geography is complimentary). Most Edcamps are locally focused, but many events draw attendees from multiple states and school districts.

Running a regional event is almost exactly the same as running an in-house Edcamp event. There are just a few additional items to consider:

- Recruiting a team that represents many schools and districts is helpful.
- Securing a venue large enough for a regional event may require some homework.
- Promoting your event is key to ensuring a good turnout.
- Fundraising might be needed to cover incurred costs.
- Accessing help via the Edcamp Foundation can jumpstart the process.

RECRUITING A DIVERSE TEAM

The more diverse your regional Edcamp organizing team, the more access you'll have to resources and educators. Most regional event teams have between five to twelve people on them from a variety of different schools and districts. Ideally, most of your team previously attended an Edcamp. If you're lucky, some might even have helped plan one. However, the most important team member qualification is passion; ages, educational backgrounds, and professional levels simply don't matter.

Edcamps came of age at the same time as social media, so it's natural that social networks often play a powerful role in the creation of regional Edcamp organizing teams. It's very common for someone interested in running an Edcamp to canvas their social networks to find like-minded educators interested in helping out with the event. No social network? No problem! Local resources, like educational services agencies are also fantastic sources for teammates.

SECURING A VENUE LARGE ENOUGH TO ACCOMMODATE REGIONAL ATTENDANCE

Regional Edcamp events typically require a relatively large space. In many cases, your best option is to hold the Edcamp at a school where a member of the organizing team works.

Check with your district administrators, school leaders, or local university connections to get started.

Remember, providing space is a pretty significant request. If you had to rent a commercial space, for example, at a hotel/conference center, the cost could easily run into the thousands of dollars. Since you are asking for use of the space for free, the venue becomes the first (and most important) sponsor of your regional Edcamp event.

Why would a school, college, or university want to provide space for your event? Here are a few reasons:

- **Free Publicity:** Edcamps are GREAT showcases of school campuses, particularly those with significant investments in technological infrastructure.

- **Thought Leadership:** Edcamps are progressive, and hosting an Edcamp positions an organization as an educational thought leader.

- **Offers Free, Easy-to-Attend Professional Development for In-House Staff:** Hosting an Edcamp means teachers local to that district or university have an instant connection to the event. While getting staff to attend professional development on their own time can be problematic from a contractual standpoint, promoting it on a VOLUNTARY basis can be (and has been) very beneficial to school communities.

If decision-makers at your potential venues are not familiar with Edcamps, you may have to educate them on both the Edcamp mission and the values that Edcamps provide. Face-to-face meetings with potential venue hosts can be critical during this early stage in the process.

PROMOTING YOUR EVENT

Promoting your event should take place using a variety of channels, but it's best to begin by creating a digital home for your event. The Edcamp Foundation provides free Wiki pages for all events via the Edcamp Wiki: http://Edcamp.wikispaces.com. All you need to do is request to "join" the wiki and you can get started with a basic page that lists your event, the date, the organizers and more. Many events also create their own websites.

Getting the word out via traditional channels is important as well. Design a flyer and send it to school districts, or educational services agencies in your area. District leadership can often provide insight into the best channels for spreading the word about your Edcamp event.

Promoting your event is important. Because educators are very busy, it's typical for Edcamp events to have about a 50 percent attrition rate on the day of the event. So, be sure to register about twice as many people as you'd like to have at your event.

FUNDRAISING

Edcamps must be free to participants. Therefore, funding is sometimes needed to host a regional event. However, fundraising should never corrupt the intention of the event: peer to peer learning. All fundraising must ensure that the Edcamp event maintains a "vendor-free" presence, which means that educators should not be subjected to sales pitches or pushy vendor booths during the event.

Here are some of the most common costs incurred by an Edcamp planning team:

- **Venue Services:** It may be necessary to purchase insurance, security, or custodial services before you can use a facility, even if it is donated. This can amount to hundreds of dollars. Always check with your venue donor about these items.

- **Paper goods:** Nametags, giant post-it sheets, tape, and markers are needed for signage and schedule board creation on the day of the event.

- **Food:** Although food is not required at an Edcamp, professional development is always better when coffee and breakfast are available!

- **Giveaways:** Most often, giveaways are donated by local companies or edtech startups. However, some Edcamps do provide T-shirts with their Edcamp logo or other small items to give away on the day of the event. This is completely optional.

Effective fundraising is a combination of local and social media powered communications. Local firms are more likely to provide funds for your event or goods and or services that can be raffled off at the end of the day. Many Edcamps have successfully targeted vendors in the Information Technology space, but really, any vendor that wishes to market to educators needs to know that your event is a great way to reach them. Again, connections on your fundraising team are important here. Spend time identifying, vetting, and prioritizing possible vendor sponsors and reach out to them EARLY in the process. Firms often need months to approve expenditures. Giving them time shows you respect their decision-making process. Reach out to these targets first.

You can also get ideas for vendors to approach by looking at the "Sponsor" pages from other Edcamps, particularly other events near your area. See the "Complete Edcamp Calendar" on the Edcamp website to find event pages and reach out to the event organizer team first, before contacting the vendor. Ask them who they contacted, what was provided, and if they have any advice for you. Leave plenty of time to complete this task.

HELP VIA THE EDCAMP FOUNDATION

The Edcamp Foundation is a nonprofit organization that was formed by the founders of the Edcamp movement. The mission of the Edcamp foundation is to support participatory, organic professional learning for educators. To accomplish this mission, the Edcamp Foundation offers a Foundation Partner Program. This program provides free one on one assistance to any educator seeking to run an Edcamp. You can apply for this free program here: http://Edcamp.org/mini-grants/

Final Thoughts

As stated at the beginning of this text, connected learning for the adults who lead our schools is in crisis. Teachers need time and space to experiment and learn with each other. Additionally, shrinking budgets and calendar constraints limit what schools and districts can do to remedy this problem. Edcamp events, professional learning events created by teachers for teachers, are one small solution to this larger problem. The Edcamp experience provides every teacher with increased access to colleagues, discussions, and technical and professional content as a result. Every teacher who runs a successful Edcamp event or Edcamp session builds and strengthens their expertise in the teaching profession, scaling access to interactive professional development for all educators.

Running an Edcamp is easy. It can be done with little to no resources, and it does not require a lot of planning. The best Edcamps are those where the attendees truly take control of the day and the learning. While the concept might feel uncomfortable or scary at first, seeing that schedule board fill up for the first time is truly magical. You'll be amazed at the diversity of interests and expertise that can be crowd-sourced from familiar colleagues and new friends.

For many educators, Edcamps are only the beginning of the journey. The connections that people make at an Edcamp continue long into the future. Whether it's through informal follow-up events, blog posts, or Twitter chats, Edcampers tend to continue learning with their new colleagues. This "long tail" of learning makes any Edcamp a truly inspiring, transformative experience. Just check out the #Edcamp on Twitter to see what's cooking!

Connecting to the Edcamp movement allows you to be part of something bigger than yourself; it allows you to empower yourself and others to refine their practice. The advent of the Internet makes this easier and more practical than ever before. We can share information and conversations effortlessly as we learn together, either at face-to-face events, or in digital spaces between events.

Connected learning is here to stay. Prepare yourself, your colleagues, and in turn, your students, for the challenging future that lies ahead. Use Edcamps to provide a platform for teachers to connect, innovate, and solve pressing problems around their practice.

Join the movement!

Connect. Engage. Unlearn. Relearn. Edcamp.

References and Further Reading

Beglau, M., Craig-Hare, J., Foltos, L., Gann, K., James, J., Jobe, H., Knight, J., & Smith, B. (2011). *Technology, coaching, and community: Power partners for improved professional development in primary and secondary education* (ISTE White Paper). Retrieved from www.iste.org/news/11–06–29/New _White_Paper_New_Standards_for_Technology_Coaching_Debut_at_ ISTE_2011.aspx

Bloom, B. S. (1956). *Taxonomy of educational objectives: Book 1.* New York: Addison-Wesley.

Boule, M. (2011). *Mob rule learning: Camps, unconferences, and trashing the talking head.* San Francisco, CA: Independent Publishers Group.

Bransford, J. D., Brown, A. L., Cocking, R. R., Donovan, M. S., & Pellegrino, J. W. (2000). *How people learn: Brain, mind, experience, and school.* Washington, DC: National Academies Press.

DeWitt, P. (2014, February 28). Why our edcamp failed [Web blog post]. *Education Week, Finding Common Ground.* Retrieved from http://blogs .edweek.org/edweek/finding_common_ground/2013/02/why_our_ edcamp_failed.html

Dufour, R., & Marzano, R. J. (2011). *Leaders of learning: How district, school, and classroom leaders improve student achievement.* New York: Solution Tree.

Gulamhussein, A. (2013). *Teaching the teachers: Effective professional development in an era of high stakes accountability.* Washington, DC: National School Boards Association.

Mazza, J. (2012, August 27). Edcamp comes to Knapp elementary—Part 1. *Lead Learner.* Retrieved from http://www.leadlearner.com/edcamp-comes-to-knapp-elementary-part-1/

Perkins, D. N. (2010). *Making learning whole: How seven principles of teaching can transform education.* New York: Wiley.

Puspitowardhani, L. (2013, August 9). My wow moment as an Edcamp organizer. *Thought. Life. Idea.* Retrieved from: http://laksmipuspi towardhani.weebly.com/1/post/2013/08/my-wow-moment-as-an-edcamp-organizer.html

Richardson, W., & Mancabelli, R. (2011). *Personal learning networks: Using the power of connections to transform education.* Bloomington, IN: Solution Tree.

Swanson, K. (2012). *Professional learning in the digital age: An educator's guide to user generated learning.* New York: Eye on Education.

Swanson, K., & Leanness, A. (2012). *Edcamp: A qualitative exploration.* Retrieved from http://Edcamp.org/2012/07/Edcamp-a-qualitative-exploration-whitepaper/

Swiak, H. (2013, September 18). I think we've created an Edcamp working group. *21st Century Classroom: The Amaryllis*. Retrieved from: http://www.heidiswiak.com/2013/09/i-think-weve-created-Edcamp-working.html

Wheeler, S. (2012, March 5). #Edcampcolumbus reflection. *Teaching Humans*. Retrieved from: http://teachinghumans.blogspot.com/2012/03/Edcamp columbus-reflection.html

Yen, C. (2013, October 4). Mystery location calls/global read aloud. *Yen4 Teaching*. Retrieved from: http://yen4teaching.blogspot.com/2013/10/mystery-location-calls-global-read-aloud.html

Yoon, K. S. (2007). *Reviewing the evidence on how professional development affects student achievement*. Washington, DC: US Department of Education. Retrieved from http://ies.ed.gov/ncee/edlabs/regions/southwest/pdf/rel_2007033.p

CORWIN
A SAGE Company

The Corwin logo—a raven striding across an open book— represents the union of courage and learning. Corwin is committed to improving education for all learners by publishing books and other professional development resources for those serving the field of PreK–12 education. By providing practical, hands-on materials, Corwin continues to carry out the promise of its motto: **"Helping Educators Do Their Work Better."**